Sharing Time

Focus: Materials
Information

PETER SLOAN &
SHERYL SLOAN

On Monday, John
used an overhead
projector. He
showed us some
plans for a house.

On Tuesday, Janice
used a VCR. She
showed us a video
of her party.

On Wednesday,
Leon used a slide
projector. He
showed us slides
of his trip.

4

On Thursday, Steffi used a computer. She showed us how to play a game.

On Friday, Stan used a large poster. He showed us pictures of big bridges.

Next week, our class
will perform a play.
We will go from
class to class
to perform it.

There are many ways to share things at school. What will you share with your class?